Aging Gracefully:

A Guide to Thriving in Your Golden Years

SAM CLARKE

Contents

Chapter 1: Embracing the Golden Years with Style and Grace 8

Chapter 2: Age is Just a Number: Debunking Myths about Aging 11

    Embracing a Positive Mindset 13

Chapter 3: The Science of Aging: What Really Happens to Our Bodies and Minds 15

    Biological Changes 15

    Psychological Changes 16

    Promoting Healthy Aging 18

Chapter 4: Laugh Lines and Wisdom: Finding Joy and Humor in the Aging Process 19

    The Fountain of Youth is Overrated 19

    "Senior Moments" – Laugh Them Off 20

    The Advantages of Aging 20

    The Gray Hair Debate 20

    Aging and Adventure 21

    In Conclusion 21

Chapter 5: Nutrition for the Ages: Eating Well for a Healthy and Happy Life 22

    The Building Blocks of a Balanced Diet 22

    Nutrition Tips for Aging Gracefully 23

In Conclusion 26

Chapter 6: Fitness Fundamentals: Staying Active for a Strong and Agile Body 28

The Benefits of Regular Exercise 28

Getting Started: Finding the Right Activity for You 29

Safety Tips for Exercising 30

10-Minute Exercise Program for Seniors 31

In Conclusion 32

Chapter 7: Keeping a Sharp Mind: Mental Exercises to Stay Mentally Fit 34

Why Mental Fitness Matters 34

Mental Exercises to Stay Mentally Fit 35

Tips for Making Mental Fitness a Habit 36

In Conclusion 37

Chapter 8: The Power of Connection: Building Strong Social Networks 38

Why Social Connection Matters 38

Building and Maintaining Strong Social Networks 39

Overcoming Social Isolation 40

In Conclusion 41

Chapter 9: Intergenerational Bonds: Bridging the Gap Between Young and Old 42

The Benefits of Intergenerational Connections 42

Ways to Foster Intergenerational Bonds 43

In Conclusion 45

Chapter 10: The Art of Reinvention: Embracing New Passions and Pursuits 46

Why Reinvention Matters 46

Tips for Embracing New Passions and Pursuits 47

Examples of New Passions and Pursuits 48

In Conclusion 49

Chapter 11: Aging in Place: Adapting Your Home for Comfort and Safety 50

What is Aging in Place? 50

Benefits of Aging in Place 50

Adapting Your Home for Comfort and Safety 51

Additional Considerations for Aging in Place 52

In Conclusion 53

Chapter 12: Fashion and Beauty: Styling Tips for a Timeless Look 54

Embracing Personal Style 54

Styling Tips for a Timeless Look 55

Beauty Tips for a Fabulous Look 56

In Conclusion 57

Chapter 13: Travel Tales: Exploring the World at Your Leisure 58

The Joys of Travel and Adventure 58

Tips for Planning Your Travels 59

Inspiring Travel Tales: Stories of Adventure and Discovery 60

The Solo Backpacker 61

The Unlikely Mountaineers 61

The Volunteer Voyage 61

The Artful Explorers 62

The Road Trip Warriors 62

In Conclusion 63

Chapter 14: The Gift of Giving Back: Volunteering and Community Involvement 64

The Benefits of Giving Back 64

Ways to Get Involved 65

Inspiring Stories of Giving Back: Changing Lives and Communities 66

The Green-Thumbed Gardener 66

The Tutoring Trailblazer 67

The Caring Canine Companion 67

The Food Bank Visionary 67

The Environmental Steward 68

In Conclusion 68

Chapter 15: Money Matters: Financial Planning for a Worry-Free Retirement 70

The Importance of Financial Planning 70

Tips for a Secure Financial Future 71

Resources for Financial Planning 72

In Conclusion 73

Chapter 16: Love and Romance: Keeping the Spark Alive . 74

The Benefits of a Healthy Romantic Relationship 74

Keeping the Spark Alive 75

Inspiring Stories of Lasting Love: Nurturing Romance through the Years 76

The High School Sweethearts 76

The Second Chance at Love 77

The Adventure Seekers 77

The Long-Distance Lovers 77

The Couple That Laughs Together 78

In Conclusion 78

Chapter 17: The Sandwich Generation: Balancing Care for Yourself and Loved Ones 79

The Challenges of the Sandwich Generation 79

Strategies for Balancing Care 80

Managing the Emotional Aspects of Caregiving 81

In Conclusion 82

Chapter 18: Embracing Technology: Staying Connected in the Digital Age 83

The Benefits of Embracing Technology 83

Tips for Overcoming the Digital Learning Curve 84

Resources for Staying Connected in the Digital Age 85

In Conclusion 86

Chapter 19: Mindfulness and Meditation: Cultivating Inner Peace and Resilience 87

    The Benefits of Mindfulness and Meditation 87

    Incorporating Mindfulness Practices into Your Daily Life 88

    Getting Started with Mindfulness and Meditation 89

    In Conclusion 90

Chapter 20: Conclusion: The Golden Ticket to a Fulfilling Life 91

    Embracing the Golden Years 91

    A Lifetime of Learning 92

    The Power of Community..92

    The Art of Balance 92

    Looking Ahead 92

About the Author 94

Chapter 1: Embracing the Golden Years with Style and Grace

Welcome to "Aging Gracefully: A Guide to Thriving in Your Golden Years"! This book is your trusty companion as you embark on the exciting journey of aging with confidence, humor, and a zest for life. You've earned your golden years, and it's time to shine! In this chapter, we'll lay the groundwork for a vibrant, fulfilling, and entertaining life in your later years.

We all know that aging is inevitable, but how we choose to experience it is entirely up to us. It's a time to celebrate the wealth of experience, knowledge, and wisdom we've accumulated. The golden years can be a period of incredible growth, joy, and opportunity if we approach them with the right mindset and attitude.

Aging gracefully is about recognizing and embracing the unique qualities that come with growing older. It's about living life to the fullest, nurturing our physical and mental well-being, and staying connected to the people and activities that bring us joy. It's about adapting to change, taking on new challenges, and finding happiness in every stage of life.

To help you thrive in your golden years, this book will cover various topics, from debunking myths about aging to exploring the science behind the process. We'll discuss the importance of nutrition, fitness, and mental exercises to keep you feeling your best. You'll learn about the power of social connections, intergenerational bonds, and embracing new passions and pursuits.

You'll discover how to adapt your home for comfort and safety, while still expressing your personal style. We'll also delve into the world of fashion, beauty, and travel, showing you that you can look fabulous and explore new adventures at any age. We'll provide guidance on financial planning, love and romance, and the unique challenges of the sandwich generation.

Throughout this journey, we'll keep things entertaining, sharing humorous anecdotes, witty insights, and heart-warming stories to keep you engaged and inspired. After all, laughter is the best medicine, and a healthy dose of humor can do wonders for our outlook on life.

As you read through these chapters, remember that the golden years are a time to celebrate your accomplishments, embrace change, and look forward to the future with optimism and enthusiasm. You've earned this time in your life, so make the most of it!

Let's embark on this journey together, with style, grace, and a sense of humor. Your golden years await – let's make them shine!

Chapter 2: Age is Just a Number: Debunking Myths about Aging

In this chapter, we'll explore some common myths and misconceptions about aging and set the record straight. By dispelling these myths, we can embrace a more positive and empowering mindset, allowing us to thrive in our golden years.

Myth 1: Aging means physical and mental decline.

While it's true that our bodies and minds undergo changes as we age, it's important to remember that decline is not inevitable. With proper nutrition, regular exercise, and mental stimulation, we can maintain our physical and cognitive health well into our later years.

Myth 2: Older people are unhappy and lonely.

Happiness and life satisfaction are not solely determined by age. Many older adults report high levels of contentment, as they have more time for leisure activities, social connections, and pursuing personal interests. By staying active and engaged, we can continue to find joy and fulfilment in our golden years.

Myth 3: Older adults are unproductive and a burden on society.

This myth couldn't be further from the truth. Older adults contribute significantly to society through their experience, wisdom, and skills. Many continue to work, volunteer, and actively participate in their communities, making valuable contributions to the lives of others.

Myth 4: Learning and personal growth stop in old age.

Our brains have the remarkable ability to continue learning and adapting throughout our lives. With a curious and open mindset, we can continue to explore new interests, acquire new skills, and grow as individuals, regardless of age.

Myth 5: Aging means giving up your independence.

While it's true that some older adults may require assistance with certain tasks, many maintain their independence and continue to live fulfilling lives. Through adaptations to our homes, staying connected to support networks, and utilizing available resources, we can maintain a sense of autonomy and control.

Myth 6: Romance and intimacy end with age.

Love, romance, and intimacy are not exclusive to the young. Many older adults continue to enjoy healthy and satisfying romantic relationships, maintaining strong emotional connections and discovering new ways to express their love and affection.

Embracing a Positive Mindset

Now that we've debunked some common myths about aging, it's important to cultivate a positive mindset to make the most of our golden years. Here are some tips for embracing a healthy outlook on aging:

1. Focus on the positives: Instead of dwelling on the challenges of aging, celebrate the wisdom, experience, and personal growth that come with each passing year.

2. Adopt an attitude of gratitude: Practice gratitude daily by appreciating the simple pleasures in life, the love of family and friends, and the opportunities that come your way.

3. Stay curious and open-minded: Embrace new experiences, interests, and learning opportunities to keep your mind sharp and engaged.

4. Foster resilience: Cultivate the ability to bounce back from setbacks and adapt to change with grace and optimism.

5. Surround yourself with positive influences: Connect with like-minded individuals who share your zest for life and can support you on your journey.

By debunking the myths surrounding aging and embracing a positive mindset, we can face our golden years with confidence, curiosity, and joy. Remember, age is just a number – it's how we choose to live our lives that truly matters.

Chapter 3: The Science of Aging: What Really Happens to Our Bodies and Minds

In this chapter, we'll delve into the fascinating world of the science of aging, exploring the biological and psychological changes that occur as we grow older. Understanding these changes can help us better appreciate the aging process and equip us with the knowledge to maintain our health and well-being.

Biological Changes

1. Cellular aging: As we age, our cells undergo changes, such as a decrease in the efficiency of cellular repair processes, accumulation of waste products, and a decline in the ability to divide and regenerate. These changes can contribute to the development of age-related diseases and conditions.

2. Hormonal shifts: Hormone levels fluctuate with age, leading to changes in various bodily functions. For example, menopause in women results from a decline in estrogen production, while men may experience a gradual decrease in testosterone levels.

3. Muscle and bone changes: Muscle mass tends to decrease with age, which can lead to reduced strength and mobility. Bone density also declines, increasing the risk of fractures and osteoporosis.

4. Cardiovascular system: The heart's efficiency may decline as we age, leading to a reduced ability to pump blood and deliver oxygen to the body. Blood vessels may also become less flexible, contributing to an increased risk of hypertension and other cardiovascular issues.

5. Cognitive changes: While some age-related cognitive decline is normal, the extent and progression can vary widely among individuals. Factors such as genetics, lifestyle choices, and overall health can play a significant role in determining how well our brains age.

Psychological Changes

1. Emotional well-being: Many older adults report an increased sense of well-being and emotional stability, as they have developed effective coping strategies and have a greater appreciation for life's experiences.

2. Wisdom and perspective: With age often comes a greater understanding of ourselves and the world around us, leading to enhanced problem-solving abilities, empathy, and perspective.

3. Social connections: As we age, our social networks may shift and evolve, with some relationships deepening while others may fade. Maintaining strong social connections is essential for our emotional well-being and overall health.

4. Life transitions: Retirement, empty nest syndrome, and the loss of loved ones are common life transitions that can affect our emotional and psychological well-being. Adapting to these changes and finding new sources of meaning and purpose can help us navigate these transitions with resilience.

Promoting Healthy Aging

Now that we understand the biological and psychological changes that occur with age, we can take steps to promote healthy aging:

1. Maintain a balanced diet: Eating nutrient-dense foods can support cellular health, hormone regulation, and overall well-being.

2. Stay physically active: Regular exercise can help preserve muscle mass, bone density, and cardiovascular health.

3. Engage in mental exercises: Challenging the brain through puzzles, games, and learning can help maintain cognitive function.

4. Cultivate social connections: Nurture relationships with family, friends, and community members to stay emotionally connected and supported.

5. Prioritize self-care: Make time for relaxation, stress reduction, and activities that bring joy and meaning to your life.

By understanding the science behind the aging process, we can take control of our health and well-being, allowing us to thrive in our golden years. It's never too late to make positive changes and embrace a healthy lifestyle that supports our bodies and minds as we age.

Chapter 4: Laugh Lines and Wisdom: Finding Joy and Humor in the Aging Process

In this chapter, we'll explore the importance of finding joy and humor in the aging process. Embracing the beauty and wisdom that come with age can help us maintain a positive outlook and thrive in our golden years. To celebrate this journey, we'll share a few anecdotes and humorous stories that highlight the lighter side of aging.

The Fountain of Youth is Overrated

Have you ever heard the saying, "Youth is wasted on the young"? As we grow older, we often come to appreciate the wisdom and perspective that age brings. While we may not have the energy of our younger selves, we have a treasure trove of life experiences that have shaped our character and enriched our lives. So next time you hear someone reminiscing about their youth, just remember that growing older has its perks too!

"Senior Moments" – Laugh Them Off
We've all had those moments when we walk into a room and completely forget why we entered, or when we can't recall where we left our keys. Instead of fretting over these so-called "senior moments," let's embrace them with humor. Laughing off these memory lapses not only reduces stress, but it also reminds us that we're all human and no one is perfect. Besides, who doesn't enjoy a good laugh?

The Advantages of Aging
As we age, we gain the privilege of a few perks that come with experience. For instance, have you ever noticed how older adults seem to have a special talent for storytelling? With years of experience under their belts, they can captivate an audience with tales of adventure, love, and life lessons learned. And let's not forget the senior discounts – who doesn't love a bargain?

The Gray Hair Debate
Some people see grey hair as a sign of wisdom and embrace it fully, while others spend countless hours and dollars trying to hide it. In reality, grey hair can be a beautiful and natural part of the aging process. So, whether you decide to let your silver locks shine or continue to experiment with various hair colors, remember to enjoy the process and do what makes you feel your best!

Aging and Adventure

Who says adventure is reserved for the young? Many older adults are embracing their golden years by trying new activities, traveling to exotic destinations, or even learning to skydive! Remember, age is just a number, and it's never too late to step out of your comfort zone and embark on a new adventure.

In Conclusion

Finding joy and humor in the aging process can help us maintain a positive outlook and embrace the beauty and wisdom that come with age. By celebrating our accomplishments, laughing at life's little hiccups, and staying open to new experiences, we can truly thrive in our golden years.

So, wear your laugh lines with pride, share your wisdom with others, and don't be afraid to embark on new adventures. After all, aging gracefully is all about living life to the fullest and finding joy in every stage of the journey.

Chapter 5: Nutrition for the Ages: Eating Well for a Healthy and Happy Life

In this chapter, we'll explore the importance of a balanced diet for our physical and mental well-being as we age. Maintaining proper nutrition is crucial for staying healthy, energetic, and mentally sharp, allowing us to make the most of our golden years.

The Building Blocks of a Balanced Diet

A balanced diet consists of a variety of foods that provide the essential nutrients our bodies need to function optimally. These nutrients include:

1. Protein: Critical for maintaining muscle mass and supporting immune function, proteins are found in lean meats, poultry, fish, beans, legumes, nuts, and dairy products.

2. Carbohydrates: Our body's primary source of energy, carbohydrates can be found in whole grains, fruits, vegetables, and legumes.

3. Healthy fats: Essential for brain health and the absorption of certain vitamins, healthy fats can be found in olive oil, avocados, nuts, seeds, and fatty fish.

4. Vitamins and minerals: Crucial for overall health and well-being, vitamins and minerals can be found in a variety of fruits, vegetables, whole grains, and lean proteins.

5. Fibre: Important for digestive health and maintaining a healthy weight, fibre is found in whole grains, fruits, vegetables, and legumes.

6. Water: Staying hydrated is essential for maintaining healthy bodily functions, including digestion, circulation, and temperature regulation.

Nutrition Tips for Aging Gracefully

As we age, our nutritional needs and preferences may change. Here are some tips to help you maintain a healthy and balanced diet:

1. Prioritize whole foods: Focus on consuming nutrient-dense, whole foods, such as fruits, vegetables, lean proteins, whole grains, and healthy fats.

2. Pay attention to portion sizes: To maintain a healthy weight, be mindful of portion sizes and avoid overeating.

3. Stay hydrated: Drink plenty of water throughout the day to support healthy digestion and prevent dehydration.

4. Limit processed foods: Reduce your intake of processed foods, which can be high in sodium, unhealthy fats, and added sugars.

5. Listen to your body: Pay attention to your hunger and fullness cues, and adjust your food intake accordingly.

6. Supplement when necessary: Consult with your healthcare provider about any necessary dietary supplements, such as vitamin D or calcium, to ensure you're meeting your nutritional needs.

7. Don't forget about flavor: As our taste buds may change with age, experiment with herbs, spices, and other flavorings to make your meals more enjoyable and satisfying.

8. Enjoy meals with others: Sharing meals with friends and family can make eating more enjoyable and provide opportunities for social connection.

A balanced diet is essential for maintaining physical and mental health, especially as we age. In this chapter, we'll explore 10 simple and healthy recipes that are suitable for seniors. These recipes are easy to prepare, nutritious, and delicious, making it easy for seniors to maintain a healthy diet.

1. Baked Salmon: Brush salmon fillets with olive oil, sprinkle with salt and pepper, and bake at 400°F/200°C for 12-15 minutes. Serve with steamed vegetables and a side salad for a healthy and satisfying meal.

2. Greek Yogurt Parfait: Layer Greek yogurt, fresh berries, and granola in a glass or bowl for a delicious and protein-packed breakfast or snack.

3. Chicken and Vegetable Stir-Fry: Sauté chicken breast, broccoli, bell peppers, and onions in a wok or skillet with soy sauce and garlic. Serve over brown rice for a filling and healthy meal.

4. Quinoa Salad: Cook quinoa according to package instructions and mix with chopped vegetables, such as cucumber, tomatoes, and bell peppers. Toss with lemon juice and olive oil for a refreshing and nutritious salad.

5. Omelette with Spinach and Mushrooms: Whisk eggs with a splash of milk, and cook in a nonstick skillet with spinach and mushrooms. Top with grated cheese and serve with whole-grain toast for a satisfying and protein-packed breakfast.

6. Turkey Chili: Cook ground turkey, onions, and garlic in a pot with canned tomatoes, kidney beans, and chili powder. Simmer for 20-30 minutes and serve with whole-grain crackers or cornbread for a comforting and healthy meal.

7. Broiled Grapefruit: Cut a grapefruit in half and sprinkle with brown sugar and cinnamon. Broil for 5-7 minutes until golden brown and serve as a light and refreshing dessert.

8. Sweet Potato and Black Bean Enchiladas: Bake sweet potatoes in the oven and mash with black beans, onions, and spices. Roll the mixture in corn tortillas and bake with enchilada sauce and grated cheese for a delicious and nutritious vegetarian meal.

9. Greek Salad: Toss chopped lettuce, cucumbers, tomatoes, and feta cheese with lemon juice and olive oil for a refreshing and nutritious salad.

10. Lentil Soup: Cook lentils with onions, garlic, and vegetables such as carrots and celery in a pot with vegetable broth. Simmer for 20-30 minutes and serve with whole-grain bread for a comforting and healthy meal.

By incorporating these simple and healthy recipes into their diet, seniors can maintain a balanced and nutritious diet, supporting their physical and mental well-being. It's important to remember to consult with a healthcare provider or nutritionist to ensure that any dietary changes are safe and appropriate for individual needs and health conditions.

In Conclusion

Proper nutrition is vital for maintaining our physical and mental well-being as we age. By focusing on a balanced diet, staying hydrated, and enjoying flavorful, nutrient-dense meals, we can support our overall health and enjoy a vibrant, fulfilling life in our golden years.

Remember, it's never too late to make positive changes to your diet and lifestyle. Embrace the journey and discover the joys of eating well for a healthy, happy life.

Chapter 6: Fitness Fundamentals: Staying Active for a Strong and Agile Body

In this chapter, we'll explore the importance of engaging in regular physical activity to maintain strength, flexibility, and balance as we age. Staying active is crucial for promoting overall health, enhancing mobility, and preserving our independence.

The Benefits of Regular Exercise

Regular physical activity offers numerous benefits for older adults, including:

1. Improved muscle strength: Strength training can help counteract the natural decline in muscle mass that occurs with age, helping to maintain our ability to perform everyday tasks.

2. Enhanced bone density: Weight-bearing exercises, such as walking, jogging, or dancing, can help

preserve bone density and reduce the risk of osteoporosis.

3. Better balance and flexibility: Exercises that focus on balance and flexibility, such as yoga or tai chi, can help reduce the risk of falls and improve overall mobility.

4. Increased cardiovascular health: Aerobic activities, such as swimming or cycling, can help maintain a healthy heart and improve circulation.

5. Boosted cognitive function: Regular exercise has been linked to better brain health and a reduced risk of cognitive decline.

6. Improved mental well-being: Physical activity can help reduce stress, improve mood, and enhance overall quality of life.

Getting Started: Finding the Right Activity for You

To reap the benefits of regular exercise, it's essential to find activities that you enjoy and that match your fitness level. Here are some suggestions for incorporating physical activity into your daily routine:

1. Walking: One of the simplest and most accessible forms of exercise, walking can be easily adjusted to match your fitness level and can be done anywhere.

2. Swimming: A low-impact, full-body workout, swimming is an excellent option for older adults looking to improve cardiovascular health and maintain joint flexibility.

3. Yoga or tai chi: These gentle practices can help improve balance, flexibility, and mental focus while reducing stress and promoting relaxation.

4. Strength training: Using resistance bands, dumbbells, or even your body weight, strength training exercises can help maintain muscle mass and bone density.

5. Group classes: Many fitness centres and community centres offer group exercise classes specifically designed for older adults, such as water aerobics, dance classes, or gentle stretching sessions.

6. Outdoor activities: Gardening, hiking, or playing with your grandchildren are all enjoyable ways to stay active while enjoying the great outdoors.

Safety Tips for Exercising

Before beginning any new exercise program, consult with your healthcare provider to ensure it's appropriate for your current health and fitness level. Keep the following safety tips in mind as you start your fitness journey:

1. Start slowly: Gradually build up the intensity and duration of your workouts to reduce the risk of injury.

2. Listen to your body: Pay attention to your body's signals and adjust your exercise routine accordingly. If something doesn't feel right, stop and seek professional guidance.

3. Warm-up and cool down: Begin each workout with a gentle warm-up, and end with a cool-down period to help prevent injury and promote flexibility.

4. Stay hydrated: Drink water before, during, and after exercising to ensure proper hydration.

5. Wear appropriate footwear: Choose supportive, well-fitting shoes that are suitable for your chosen activity to reduce the risk of injury.

Regular exercise is essential to maintaining physical health, especially as we age. However, it can be challenging to know where to start or how to fit exercise into a busy schedule. In this chapter, we'll explore some simple and effective exercises that can be done in just 10 minutes, making it easy for seniors to incorporate physical activity into their daily routines.

10-Minute Exercise Program for Seniors:

1. Warm-up (2 minutes) Start with a gentle warm-up to prepare your body for exercise. March in place or take a brisk walk around the house for two minutes.

2. Chair Squats (2 minutes) sit in a sturdy chair with your feet flat on the ground and your hands resting on your thighs. Stand up slowly, using your leg muscles to lift yourself out of the chair. Hold for a few seconds, then lower yourself back down to a seated position. Repeat for two minutes.

3. Wall Push-Ups (2 minutes) stand facing a wall with your feet shoulder-width apart. Place your palms flat

on the wall at chest height, shoulder-width apart. Bend your elbows and lean forward, allowing your body to come towards the wall. Push back to your starting position. Repeat for two minutes.

4. Leg Raises (2 minutes) sit in a chair with your feet flat on the ground and your hands resting on the chair arms. Lift one leg off the ground, keeping it straight, and hold for a few seconds before lowering it back down. Repeat with the other leg. Alternate between legs for two minutes.

5. Cool Down (2 minutes) Finish your workout with a cool-down to bring your heart rate back to normal. March in place or walk slowly around the house for two minutes.

By following this simple 10-minute exercise program, seniors can improve their strength, flexibility, and balance. It's important to remember that everyone's fitness level is different, so it's essential to listen to your body and start slowly. Over time, you can increase the duration and intensity of your workout to continue challenging yourself and achieving your fitness goals.

In Conclusion
Staying active is vital for maintaining a strong and agile body as we age. By engaging in regular physical activity, we can improve our overall health, enhance our mobility, and preserve our independence. Remember, it's never too late to

start a fitness routine – embrace the journey and discover the joys of staying active in your golden years.

Chapter 7: Keeping a Sharp Mind: Mental Exercises to Stay Mentally Fit

In this chapter, we'll discuss the importance of stimulating and challenging the brain to stay mentally fit as we age. Engaging in mental exercises, such as puzzles, games, and learning, can help maintain cognitive function and promote overall brain health.

Why Mental Fitness Matters

Just as physical exercise is essential for maintaining a healthy body, mental exercise is crucial for preserving our cognitive abilities. Mental fitness can:

1. Improve memory: Challenging the brain can enhance our ability to recall information and form new memories.

2. Boost problem-solving skills: Mental exercises can help sharpen our critical thinking and problem-solving abilities.

3. Enhance concentration: Regularly engaging in activities that require focus can improve our ability to concentrate on tasks.

4. Support brain health: Mental stimulation has been linked to a reduced risk of cognitive decline and conditions such as dementia and Alzheimer's disease.

5. Increase self-esteem and confidence: Learning new skills and accomplishing mental challenges can boost our self-esteem and confidence.

Mental Exercises to Stay Mentally Fit

Here are some ideas for mental exercises that can help keep your brain sharp and engaged:

1. Puzzles and brainteasers: Sudoku, crossword puzzles, and other brainteasers are excellent ways to give your brain a workout. These activities can improve memory, concentration, and problem-solving skills.

2. Reading: Reading books, articles, or even engaging in online discussions can help expand your knowledge, stimulate your imagination, and improve your vocabulary and comprehension skills.

3. Learning a new skill: Whether it's learning a new language, taking up a musical instrument, or mastering a new craft, acquiring new skills challenges

the brain and encourages the formation of new neural connections.

4. Playing games: Board games, card games, and even video games can provide cognitive stimulation and improve various mental skills, such as memory, decision-making, and strategic thinking.

5. Engaging in creative pursuits: Activities like painting, drawing, writing, or playing a musical instrument can enhance creativity and stimulate different areas of the brain.

6. Staying socially active: Social interaction is essential for mental well-being and can help keep the brain engaged through conversation, shared experiences, and problem-solving.

7. Practicing mindfulness and meditation: Regular mindfulness practice, such as meditation or deep breathing exercises, can help improve focus, reduce stress, and enhance overall mental well-being.

Tips for Making Mental Fitness a Habit

To make mental fitness a regular part of your routine, consider the following tips:

1. Set aside time: Dedicate a specific time each day for mental exercises, just as you would for physical exercise.

2. Choose activities you enjoy: Select mental exercises that you find engaging and enjoyable to increase the likelihood of sticking with your routine.

3. Mix it up: Vary your mental exercises to challenge different areas of the brain and keep things interesting.

4. Involve others: Engage with friends or family members in mental exercises or games to make the activity more enjoyable and foster social connections.

In Conclusion

Keeping a sharp mind is essential for maintaining our cognitive abilities and overall brain health as we age. By engaging in regular mental exercises, such as puzzles, games, and learning, we can stay mentally fit and enjoy a vibrant, fulfilling life in our golden years. Remember, it's never too late to start challenging your brain – embrace the journey and discover the joys of mental fitness.

Chapter 8: The Power of Connection: Building Strong Social Networks

In this chapter, we'll explore the importance of building strong social networks as we age. Nurturing relationships with family, friends, and community members not only provides us with social support but also contributes to our overall well-being and happiness in our golden years.

Why Social Connection Matters

Maintaining strong social connections is essential for a fulfilling and happy life as we age. Here are some of the key benefits of staying socially connected:

1. Improved mental health: Regular social interaction can help reduce feelings of loneliness and isolation, improve mood, and decrease the risk of depression.

2. Enhanced cognitive function: Engaging in conversations and social activities can stimulate the brain and help maintain cognitive function.

3. Better physical health: Socially active individuals tend to have better physical health, possibly due to the motivation and support provided by their social network.

4. Increased longevity: Research has shown that having strong social connections is linked to a longer lifespan.

5. Emotional support: A strong social network can provide emotional support during challenging times, helping us navigate the ups and downs of life.

Building and Maintaining Strong Social Networks

Here are some tips for building and maintaining strong social connections in your golden years:

1. Stay in touch with friends and family: Regularly reach out to your loved ones through phone calls, video chats, or social media to keep your relationships strong.

2. Join clubs or groups: Participate in clubs or organizations that align with your interests, such as hobby groups, book clubs, or gardening clubs.

3. Volunteer your time: Volunteering for local charities or community organizations is a great way to meet new people and give back to your community.

4. Attend social events: Take advantage of social events in your community, such as neighbourhood gatherings, holiday celebrations, or cultural events.

5. Stay physically active with others: Participate in group exercise classes or walking groups to stay active while connecting with others.

6. Be open to new friendships: Keep an open mind and be willing to form new friendships with people of all ages and backgrounds.

7. Offer support to others: Be there for your friends and family members when they need support, and don't be afraid to ask for help when you need it.

8. Maintain a positive attitude: A positive attitude can make you more approachable and help attract others to you, making it easier to form and maintain connections.

Overcoming Social Isolation

As we age, we may face obstacles that make it challenging to maintain social connections. Here are some strategies for overcoming social isolation:

1. Reach out for support: If you're feeling isolated, don't hesitate to reach out to friends, family, or healthcare professionals for support and guidance.

2. Stay engaged in your community: Attend local events, join clubs, or volunteer to stay connected with your community and meet new people.

3. Embrace technology: Learn how to use technology, such as social media or video chat platforms, to stay in touch with friends and family members who live far away.

4. Be proactive: Take the initiative to organize social events or gatherings with friends, family, or neighbours.

In Conclusion

Building strong social networks is essential for thriving in our golden years. By nurturing relationships with family, friends, and community members, we can benefit from the social support, emotional well-being, and cognitive stimulation that come from staying connected. Embrace the power of connection and discover the joys of a socially active and fulfilling life in your golden years.

Chapter 9: Intergenerational Bonds: Bridging the Gap Between Young and Old

In this chapter, we'll explore the importance of fostering understanding, respect, and collaboration between different generations. Building intergenerational bonds can enrich our lives, promote empathy, and create a sense of community that spans across age groups.

The Benefits of Intergenerational Connections

There are numerous benefits to fostering connections between young and old, including:

1. Wisdom sharing: Older adults can share their experiences, knowledge, and life lessons with younger generations, while young people can share their perspectives and fresh ideas.

2. Emotional support: Intergenerational connections can provide emotional support and encouragement to both young and old, creating a sense of belonging and understanding.

3. Skill exchange: Younger and older individuals can learn from one another by sharing their unique skills and talents.

4. Breaking down stereotypes: Building connections between generations can help break down age-related stereotypes and promote mutual respect.

5. Social engagement: Intergenerational activities provide opportunities for socialization and community involvement.

6. Legacy-building: Older adults can pass down their values, traditions, and family history to younger generations, preserving their legacy for future generations.

Ways to Foster Intergenerational Bonds

Here are some ideas for promoting intergenerational connections in your life:

1. Family gatherings: Organize regular family gatherings that bring together relatives of all ages, providing opportunities for conversation, bonding, and shared experiences.

2. Mentoring programs: Participate in mentoring programs, either as a mentor or mentee, to build connections and share wisdom across generations.

3. Intergenerational volunteer opportunities: Seek out volunteer opportunities that involve both young and old, such as community gardening projects, tutoring programs, or senior center activities.

4. Educational workshops or classes: Attend workshops or classes that cater to a diverse age range, such as art classes or language courses, to learn and grow together.

5. Storytelling: Encourage storytelling sessions where older adults can share their life experiences and younger generations can share their dreams and aspirations.

6. Intergenerational living arrangements: Consider living arrangements that promote intergenerational interaction, such as shared housing or co-housing communities.

7. Collaborative projects: Engage in collaborative projects, such as crafting, cooking, or gardening, that allow for skill sharing and teamwork between generations.

Overcoming Challenges

Building intergenerational bonds can sometimes be challenging due to generational differences, communication barriers, or preconceived notions. Here are some strategies to help overcome these challenges:

1. Practice active listening: Make an effort to truly listen and understand the perspectives of others, regardless of their age.

2. Show respect and empathy: Treat everyone with respect and empathy, acknowledging their unique experiences and viewpoints.

3. Be open-minded: Approach intergenerational relationships with an open mind, ready to learn from others and embrace different perspectives.

4. Communicate effectively: Adapt your communication style to ensure it is clear and appropriate for the individual with whom you are interacting.

In Conclusion

Intergenerational bonds can significantly enrich our lives by fostering understanding, respect, and collaboration between generations. By actively seeking opportunities to connect with people of all ages, we can create a sense of community that transcends generational boundaries and allows us to learn from one another's unique experiences. Embrace the power of intergenerational connections and discover the joys of bridging the gap between young and old in your golden years.

Chapter 10: The Art of Reinvention: Embracing New Passions and Pursuits

In this chapter, we'll explore the concept of reinvention and discuss how embracing new passions and pursuits can lead to personal growth and a more fulfilling life in our golden years. As we age, it's important to stay curious and open to new experiences, allowing ourselves to evolve and adapt to life's changes.

Why Reinvention Matters
Reinventing ourselves by discovering new hobbies, interests, and activities can have a significant impact on our overall well-being and happiness. Here are some reasons why reinvention matters:

1. Personal growth: Trying new things allows us to learn more about ourselves, develop new skills, and grow as individuals.

2. Adaptability: Embracing change and reinvention can help us become more adaptable and resilient in the face of life's challenges.

3. Cognitive stimulation: Engaging in new activities can keep our minds sharp and promote cognitive health.

4. Social connection: Pursuing new interests can help us expand our social circles and connect with like-minded individuals.

5. Sense of purpose: Discovering new passions can provide us with a sense of purpose and fulfilment, improving our overall well-being.

Tips for Embracing New Passions and Pursuits

Here are some strategies for embracing new passions and pursuits in your golden years:

1. Stay curious: Maintain an open mind and a curious attitude, always looking for new experiences and opportunities to learn.

2. Step out of your comfort zone: Push yourself to try new activities or pursuits that may initially feel uncomfortable or challenging.

3. Set achievable goals: Establish realistic and achievable goals for yourself, taking into account your current abilities, resources, and interests.

4. Be patient with yourself: Remember that learning and growth take time, so be patient with yourself as you explore new interests.

5. Connect with others: Seek out others who share your interests, either in person or online, to foster camaraderie and support.

6. Evaluate your interests: Periodically assess your hobbies and interests, considering whether they still bring you joy and fulfilment.

7. Stay open to change: Recognize that your interests and passions may evolve over time, and be open to adapting and changing your pursuits accordingly.

Examples of New Passions and Pursuits

Here are some ideas for new hobbies, interests, and activities to explore:

1. Learning a new language: Studying a new language can be mentally stimulating and open up opportunities for travel and cultural experiences.

2. Taking up a new sport or fitness activity: Experiment with different sports or fitness activities, such as yoga, dancing, or swimming, to find something that aligns with your interests and abilities.

3. Exploring the arts: Try your hand at painting, drawing, sculpture, or other visual arts, or delve into the world of music or theatre.

4. Engaging in community projects: Get involved in community projects, such as neighbourhood beautification initiatives, local events, or charity work.

5. Pursuing lifelong learning: Enrol in classes or attend workshops on topics that interest you, such as history, science, or philosophy.

6. Traveling: Plan trips to new destinations, either locally or internationally, to broaden your horizons and experience different cultures.

In Conclusion

The art of reinvention is an essential aspect of thriving in our golden years. By embracing new passions and pursuits, we can promote personal growth, stimulate our minds, and foster social connections. Stay curious, be open to change, and discover the joys of reinvention as you navigate your journey through your golden years.

Chapter 11: Aging in Place: Adapting Your Home for Comfort and Safety

In this chapter, we'll discuss the concept of aging in place and provide tips for adapting your home to support independence, comfort, and safety as you age. Creating a living environment that meets your needs and promotes well-being is crucial for thriving in your golden years.

What is Aging in Place?
Aging in place refers to the ability to live in one's own home and community safely, independently, and comfortably, regardless of age, income, or ability level. It involves making modifications to your living environment to accommodate your changing needs as you age.

Benefits of Aging in Place
Here are some advantages of aging in place:

1. Familiarity: Remaining in a familiar environment can provide a sense of comfort, stability, and security.

2. Independence: Aging in place allows you to maintain control over your daily routines and activities, promoting a sense of autonomy and independence.

3. Social connections: Staying in your community enables you to maintain existing social connections and continue to engage with neighbours and friends.

4. Financial considerations: In many cases, aging in place can be more cost-effective than moving to an assisted living facility or retirement home.

Adapting Your Home for Comfort and Safety

Here are some tips for adapting your home to support aging in place:

1. Evaluate your living space: Assess your current living environment to identify potential safety hazards, accessibility issues, and areas that may require modification.

2. Prevent falls: Install grab bars in the bathroom, secure rugs and carpets, and ensure that pathways are clear and well-lit to prevent falls.

3. Improve accessibility: Consider installing ramps, stairlifts, or wider doorways to improve accessibility and accommodate mobility aids such as wheelchairs or walkers.

4. Modify the bathroom: Install a walk-in shower or bathtub, a raised toilet seat, and non-slip flooring to enhance safety and convenience in the bathroom.

5. Adjust the kitchen: Make adjustments to your kitchen, such as installing pull-out shelves, lowering countertops, or adding accessible appliances, to accommodate your changing needs.

6. Plan for emergency situations: Ensure that your home is equipped with working smoke detectors, carbon monoxide detectors, and an accessible emergency exit plan.

7. Consider home automation: Install home automation technology, such as smart thermostats, lighting controls, or voice-activated devices, to make daily tasks more manageable and convenient.

8. Seek professional assistance: Consult with an aging-in-place specialist, occupational therapist, or contractor experienced in home modifications for older adults to ensure that your adaptations are safe and effective.

Additional Considerations for Aging in Place

In addition to modifying your home, consider the following aspects of aging in place:

1. Support services: Research and arrange for support services, such as in-home care, meal delivery, or transportation services, to help maintain your independence.

2. Community resources: Familiarize yourself with community resources, such as senior centres, adult day programs, and social services, to stay connected and engaged with your community.

3. Legal and financial planning: Consult with legal and financial professionals to plan for your future needs, including estate planning, long-term care insurance, and advance directives.

In Conclusion

Aging in place is an attractive option for many older adults, as it allows for continued independence, comfort, and safety in a familiar environment. By proactively adapting your home and planning for your future needs, you can create a living space that supports your well-being and enables you to thrive in your golden years.

Chapter 12: Fashion and Beauty: Styling Tips for a Timeless Look

In this chapter, we'll explore fashion and beauty tips for creating a timeless look that embraces personal style and helps you look fabulous at any age. Just because you're aging doesn't mean you can't stay stylish and feel confident in your appearance.

Embracing Personal Style

Your personal style is a reflection of your unique personality, tastes, and preferences. Embracing your personal style as you age is crucial for maintaining a sense of self-confidence and self-expression. Here are some tips for embracing your personal style:

1. Know your body: Understand your body shape and what silhouettes, cuts, and styles are most flattering on you.

2. Develop your signature look: Identify the colors, patterns, and textures that resonate with you and incorporate them into your wardrobe to create a cohesive, signature look.

3. Invest in quality pieces: Invest in high-quality, timeless pieces that will last for years and can be mixed and matched with other items in your wardrobe.

4. Stay true to yourself: Don't be afraid to express your unique personality through your clothing and accessories. Wear what makes you feel confident and comfortable.

5. Update your wardrobe: Periodically assess your wardrobe and update it with new pieces that reflect your evolving style and preferences.

Styling Tips for a Timeless Look

Here are some styling tips to help you create a timeless, ageless look:

1. Focus on fit: Make sure your clothes fit well and flatter your body shape. Tailor items if necessary to achieve the perfect fit.

2. For a classic look, invest in a few quality pieces such as a tailored suit, a crisp white dress shirt, and a pair of well-made leather shoes.

3. Accessories can also make a big difference. Consider adding a stylish watch, a classic leather belt, or a pair of sunglasses to your look.

4. Opt for comfortable footwear: Choose stylish yet comfortable shoes that provide adequate support and cushioning for your feet.

5. Layer strategically: Learn how to layer clothing effectively to create versatile, stylish outfits suitable for various weather conditions and occasions.

6. Embrace color: Don't be afraid to incorporate color into your wardrobe. Choose hues that complement your skin tone and make you feel vibrant and confident.

Beauty Tips for a Fabulous Look

In addition to fashion, maintaining a beauty routine can help you look and feel you're best at any age. Here are some beauty tips for a fabulous look for the ladies:

1. Prioritize skincare: Invest in a quality skincare routine to keep your skin looking healthy, radiant, and youthful.

2. Update your makeup: As you age, your skin tone and texture may change. Update your makeup products and techniques to enhance your natural beauty and complement your changing features.

3. Take care of your hair: Keep your hair healthy and well-groomed by getting regular trims, using nourishing hair care products, and choosing a flattering hairstyle that suits your face shape and lifestyle.

4. Don't forget your nails: Maintain well-groomed nails by keeping them clean, trimmed, and polished, if desired.

5. Practice good posture: Stand tall and maintain good posture to exude confidence and grace.

In Conclusion

Embracing personal style and looking fabulous at any age is possible by focusing on fit, choosing classic pieces, and maintaining a beauty routine. By staying true to yourself and expressing your unique personality through fashion and beauty, you can continue to feel confident and stylish in your golden years.

Chapter 13: Travel Tales: Exploring the World at Your Leisure

In this chapter, we'll delve into the joys of travel and adventure in your golden years, discussing the benefits of traveling, tips for planning your trips, and sharing inspiring travel tales that showcase the possibilities of exploration at any age.

The Joys of Travel and Adventure

Traveling during your golden years offers a unique opportunity to explore the world at your leisure, free from the constraints of work and family obligations. Here are some benefits of traveling during this stage of life:

1. Personal growth: Traveling exposes you to new cultures, experiences, and perspectives, fostering personal growth and broadening your horizons.

2. Lifelong learning: Visiting new destinations and engaging with local history, art, and customs

provides an opportunity for lifelong learning and intellectual stimulation.

3. Social connections: Traveling allows you to meet new people and forge connections with fellow travellers and locals, enriching your social life.

4. Health and well-being: Traveling can have positive effects on your mental, emotional, and physical well-being, reducing stress and promoting relaxation.

5. Sense of accomplishment: Traveling to new places and overcoming challenges associated with travel can instil a sense of accomplishment and boost self-confidence.

Tips for Planning Your Travels

Here are some tips for planning your travels during your golden years:

1. Set realistic expectations: Consider your physical abilities, interests, and budget when planning your trips, setting realistic expectations for the type of experiences and activities you can enjoy.

2. Do your research: Research your destinations thoroughly, including local customs, transportation options, and accessibility, to ensure a smooth and enjoyable trip.

3. Prioritize comfort and convenience: Opt for accommodations and transportation options that prioritize comfort and convenience, such as hotels

with amenities catered to older adults or direct flights.

4. Consult with a travel agent or specialist: Work with a travel agent or specialist who has experience planning trips for older adults and can help you navigate the logistics and accommodations specific to your needs.

5. Consider group tours or cruises: If you prefer a more structured travel experience, consider joining a group tour or cruise tailored to the interests and abilities of older adults.

6. Purchase travel insurance: Invest in travel insurance that covers medical emergencies, trip cancellations, and other unforeseen circumstances, providing peace of mind during your travels.

7. Stay connected: Keep in touch with family and friends while you're traveling, sharing your experiences and providing updates on your whereabouts for safety purposes.

Inspiring Travel Tales: Stories of Adventure and Discovery

Following are inspiring travel tales from individuals who have embraced the joys of travel and adventure in their golden years. These stories will showcase the transformative power of travel and provide a glimpse into the diverse experiences and destinations waiting to be explored.

The Solo Backpacker

Meet Jane, a 70-year-old retiree who decided to embark on a solo backpacking trip across Southeast Asia. After a fulfilling career and raising her children, Jane yearned for adventure and personal growth. Despite initial apprehensions, she pushed past her comfort zone and began a six-month journey, exploring countries like Thailand, Vietnam, and Indonesia. Along the way, she discovered her love for spicy cuisine, learned about local cultures, and made new friends from all around the world. Jane's adventure not only broadened her horizons but also reignited her passion for life.

The Unlikely Mountaineers

Tom and Linda, both in their late 60s, had always been avid hikers. But it wasn't until their retirement that they set their sights on a more ambitious goal: climbing Mount Kilimanjaro. With months of training and preparation, the couple embarked on the challenging trek. As they ascended the mountain, they were rewarded with breathtaking views and a newfound sense of accomplishment. Reaching the summit together, Tom and Linda proved that age is just a number and that determination and perseverance can conquer even the most formidable challenges.

The Volunteer Voyage

When Susan retired from her nursing career at the age of 65, she knew she wanted to continue making a difference in people's lives. That's when she discovered volunteer tourism, which allowed her to combine her love for travel with her passion for helping others. Susan joined a medical mission trip to a remote village in Central America, where she provided essential healthcare services to the local community. During her three-month stay, Susan not only experienced a new culture but also formed deep connections with the people she served, leaving an indelible impact on their lives.

The Artful Explorers

For as long as they could remember, 72-year-old Peter and his wife, Alice, had been passionate about art. To celebrate their golden anniversary, they decided to embark on an "art tour" of Europe, visiting the continent's most renowned museums and galleries. From the Louvre in Paris to the Uffizi Gallery in Florence, Peter and Alice reveled in the beauty and history of the world's greatest masterpieces. This unforgettable journey not only deepened their appreciation for art but also strengthened the bond they shared as a couple.

The Road Trip Warriors

At 68, lifelong friends Karen and Diane decided it was time for the ultimate road trip. They packed their bags, rented an RV, and set off on a three-month journey across the United States. With no set itinerary, Karen and Diane embraced the freedom of the open road, discovering hidden gems and making unforgettable memories along the way. From the breathtaking landscapes of national parks to the bustling energy of big cities, their epic road trip rekindled their spirit of adventure and reinforced the power of lifelong friendship.

These inspiring travel tales serve as a testament to the transformative experiences and personal growth that await in your golden years. Whether you're a solo adventurer, a thrill-seeker, or someone looking to give back, there's no shortage of opportunities for exploration and discovery. So go ahead, pack your bags, and embark on your own adventure – the world is waiting for you!

In Conclusion

Traveling during your golden years can be a fulfilling and enriching experience, offering opportunities for personal growth, lifelong learning, and social connection. By planning carefully and prioritizing comfort and convenience, you can discover the joys of travel and adventure, creating lasting memories and expanding your horizons as you explore the world at your leisure.

Chapter 14: The Gift of Giving Back: Volunteering and Community Involvement

In this chapter, we'll explore the importance of volunteering and community involvement in your golden years, discussing the benefits of giving back, ways to get involved, and sharing inspiring stories of individuals who have made a positive impact on others through service and philanthropy.

The Benefits of Giving Back

Volunteering and community involvement provide a sense of purpose and fulfilment, enriching your life and the lives of others. Here are some benefits of giving back during your golden years:

1. Social connections: Volunteering offers an opportunity to forge new friendships and strengthen existing relationships with like-minded individuals who share your passion for helping others.

2. Mental and emotional well-being: Giving back can boost self-esteem, alleviate stress, and promote happiness and satisfaction.

3. Personal growth: Volunteering and community involvement provide opportunities for personal growth, skill development, and learning.

4. Sense of purpose: Engaging in meaningful activities that benefit others can instil a sense of purpose and accomplishment.

5. Physical activity: Many volunteer activities involve physical activity, contributing to overall health and fitness.

Ways to Get Involved

There are countless ways to get involved in your community and make a positive impact on the lives of others. Here are some ideas to help you find the right fit:

1. Identify your passions: Reflect on your interests, skills, and values to determine the causes and activities that resonate with you.

2. Research local opportunities: Research local volunteer opportunities through community canters, non-profit organizations, or online platforms dedicated to connecting volunteers with organizations in need.

3. Share your skills: Offer your skills and expertise to organizations that could benefit from your

knowledge, such as mentoring young people, providing financial guidance, or teaching a class.

4. Join a club or organization: Participate in clubs or organizations in your community that focus on philanthropy and community service, such as Rotary Club, Lions Club, or a local gardening club.

5. Get involved in your neighbourhood: Engage with your neighbours by organizing a neighbourhood clean-up, creating a community garden, or hosting a block party.

6. Consider virtual volunteering: If you have limited mobility or prefer to volunteer from home, consider virtual volunteering opportunities, such as online tutoring or remote administrative support for non-profits.

Inspiring Stories of Giving Back: Changing Lives and Communities

These are inspiring stories of individuals who have made a positive impact on their communities through volunteering and philanthropy. These tales will demonstrate the transformative power of giving back and serve as a testament to the difference one person can make.

The Green-Thumbed Gardener

After retiring from her teaching career at 67, Mary discovered a passion for gardening. Wanting to share her love for plants and nature with others, she began volunteering at a local community garden. Over time, Mary helped transform a once-neglected plot of land into a thriving oasis, providing fresh produce for neighbourhood residents and fostering a sense of community. Her dedication and enthusiasm inspired others to join in, creating a green space that continues to nourish both the body and the soul.

The Tutoring Trailblazer

Jim, a retired engineer at 70, saw a need for tutoring and mentorship in his community's underprivileged schools. With a strong background in math and science, he decided to put his knowledge to good use by volunteering as a tutor. Over the years, Jim has helped countless students improve their grades, boost their confidence, and pursue higher education. His commitment to education and the success of the next generation has left a lasting impact on the lives of many young people.

The Caring Canine Companion

At the age of 62, Laura adopted a rescue dog named Charlie. Inspired by the bond they shared, Laura and Charlie became a certified therapy dog team, visiting hospitals, nursing homes, and schools to provide comfort and companionship to those in need. Through their gentle presence, Laura and Charlie have brought joy and solace to countless individuals, demonstrating the healing power of the human-animal bond.

The Food Bank Visionary

When Helen retired at 65, she noticed that many seniors in her community struggled with food insecurity. Determined to make a difference, she founded a food bank specifically tailored to the needs of older adults. With the help of dedicated volunteers, Helen's food bank has grown exponentially, providing nutritious meals and a support network for countless seniors in need. Her vision and tireless efforts have not only alleviated hunger but also fostered a sense of dignity and community among the food bank's patrons.

The Environmental Steward
At 71, Frank knew he wanted to leave a legacy that would benefit future generations. A lifelong nature enthusiast, he decided to start a grassroots organization dedicated to preserving and restoring local ecosystems. Over the years, Frank's organization has spearheaded numerous conservation projects, from tree planting initiatives to river clean-ups. His commitment to environmental stewardship has inspired others to join the cause, ensuring a greener and healthier future for generations to come.

These inspiring stories of giving back highlight the extraordinary impact that individuals can have on their communities and the world at large. By dedicating time, energy, and expertise to causes they care about, these individuals have demonstrated that it's never too late to make a difference. As you journey through your golden years, consider how you, too, can contribute to the well-being of others and create a legacy of lasting change.

In Conclusion
Volunteering and community involvement in your golden years can provide numerous benefits, such as promoting social connections, personal growth, and a sense of purpose. By identifying your passions and seeking out opportunities to give back, you can make a positive impact on others and enrich your own life in the process. The gift of giving back is

truly priceless, and the joy and fulfilment it brings are immeasurable.

Chapter 15: Money Matters: Financial Planning for a Worry-Free Retirement

In this chapter, we'll discuss the importance of financial planning for a worry-free retirement, covering essential aspects such as budgeting, investment strategies, and managing expenses. We'll also share tips for preparing for a secure financial future and resources to help guide you through the process.

The Importance of Financial Planning

Financial planning is crucial for ensuring a comfortable and secure retirement. Proper planning can help you maintain your desired lifestyle, cover unexpected expenses, and leave a financial legacy for your loved ones. Here are some essential aspects to consider when planning for a worry-free retirement:

1. Budgeting: Establish a realistic budget that accounts for your fixed expenses, discretionary spending, and long-term financial goals.

2. Saving and investing: Develop a savings and investment strategy that aligns with your risk tolerance and financial objectives.

3. Retirement income sources: Understand and optimize your retirement income sources, such as Social Security, pensions, and annuities.

4. Tax planning: Implement tax-efficient strategies to minimize your tax liability during retirement.

5. Estate planning: Ensure your assets are protected and distributed according to your wishes through proper estate planning, including wills, trusts, and beneficiary designations.

Tips for a Secure Financial Future

Here are some tips to help you prepare for a secure financial future and manage your expenses during retirement:

1. Start planning early: The sooner you begin planning for retirement, the more time you'll have to save, invest, and make adjustments to your financial plan.

2. Diversify your investments: Diversify your investment portfolio to spread risk and increase the potential for long-term growth.

3. Seek professional advice: Consult with a financial planner or advisor to help you develop a

comprehensive financial plan tailored to your needs and goals.

4. Monitor your progress: Regularly review your financial plan, making adjustments as needed to stay on track toward your financial objectives.

5. Downsize or relocate: Consider downsizing your home or relocating to a more affordable area to reduce your housing expenses and stretch your retirement savings further.

6. Eliminate debt: Aim to pay off high-interest debt before retiring to reduce your financial burden during retirement.

7. Take advantage of senior discounts: Many businesses and organizations offer discounts for older adults, which can help you save money on everyday expenses.

Resources for Financial Planning

There are numerous resources available to assist you with financial planning for retirement, including:

1. Financial planning books and online courses: Educate yourself on personal finance and retirement planning through books, online courses, and reputable financial websites.

2. Financial advisors: Seek the guidance of a certified financial planner or advisor who can provide personalized advice and recommendations.

3. Online tools and calculators: Use online tools and calculators to estimate your retirement savings needs, Social Security benefits, and potential investment returns.

4. Government resources: Consult resources from government agencies, such as the Social Security Administration and the Internal Revenue Service, for information on retirement income, taxes, and other financial matters.

In Conclusion

Financial planning is essential for ensuring a worry-free retirement and maintaining your desired lifestyle. By focusing on budgeting, saving, investing, and managing expenses, you can prepare for a secure financial future and enjoy your golden years with peace of mind. Remember, it's never too late to start planning and taking control of your financial well-being.

Chapter 16: Love and Romance: Keeping the Spark Alive

In this chapter, we'll explore the importance of nurturing and maintaining romantic relationships as you age. We'll discuss ways to keep the spark alive, the benefits of a healthy romantic relationship, and share inspiring stories of couples who have found lasting love in their golden years.

The Benefits of a Healthy Romantic Relationship

A strong romantic relationship can provide numerous benefits in your golden years, including:

1. Emotional support: A loving partner offers emotional support and companionship, helping to alleviate feelings of loneliness and isolation.

2. Improved mental health: Being in a healthy relationship can contribute to lower stress levels and improved overall mental health.

3. Physical health: Couples who maintain a strong emotional connection often enjoy better physical health, as they tend to engage in healthier habits and activities together.

4. Increased happiness: A fulfilling romantic relationship can lead to increased happiness and overall life satisfaction.

Keeping the Spark Alive

As you age, it's essential to nurture and maintain your romantic relationships to keep the spark alive. Here are some tips to help you achieve this:

1. Communicate openly: Open and honest communication is the foundation of any strong relationship. Share your thoughts, feelings, and concerns with your partner regularly.

2. Prioritize quality time: Spend quality time together to strengthen your emotional connection, whether it's a regular date night, a weekend getaway, or simply enjoying each other's company at home.

3. Show appreciation: Express your love and gratitude for your partner through small gestures, such as leaving a sweet note, giving a thoughtful gift, or offering a compliment.

4. Keep the romance alive: Surprise your partner with romantic gestures, such as planning a special evening, writing a heartfelt letter, or reminiscing about the early days of your relationship.

5. Be adaptable: Recognize that relationships evolve over time, and be willing to adapt to changes in your partner and your circumstances.

6. Maintain intimacy: Cultivate emotional and physical intimacy by being affectionate, sharing your feelings, and maintaining a healthy sex life.

7. Seek help if needed: If you're facing challenges in your relationship, consider seeking the guidance of a couples therapist or counsellor to help you navigate any issues and strengthen your bond.

Inspiring Stories of Lasting Love: Nurturing Romance through the Years

These inspiring stories of lasting love serve as a testament to the power of commitment, resilience, and shared experiences in maintaining a strong romantic relationship as you age. As you navigate the joys and challenges of your golden years, remember to cherish the love and connection you share with your partner, and never stop nurturing the bond that brought you together in the first place.

The High School Sweethearts

Sara and Jack fell in love as teenagers and have been inseparable ever since. Now in their 70s, the couple has faced countless challenges and joys together, from raising a family to embarking on new careers. Over the years, they have continued to prioritize their relationship, nurturing their connection through communication, shared hobbies, and regular date nights. Sara and Jack's enduring love serves as a testament to the power of commitment and the importance of growing together as a couple.

The Second Chance at Love

After losing their respective spouses, 62-year-old Maria and 65-year-old Robert never expected to find love again. But fate had other plans, and the two met by chance at a support group for widows and widowers. Over time, their shared experiences and mutual understanding blossomed into a deep love and affection. Maria and Robert's story reminds us that it's never too late to find love and that new beginnings can arise from the most challenging circumstances.

The Adventure Seekers

Lucy and George, both in their late 60s, have always shared a love for adventure and exploration. As they transitioned into retirement, they made a pact to visit a new destination every year, making cherished memories along the way. By embracing their shared passions and continually experiencing new things together, Lucy and George have maintained a strong and vibrant connection throughout their golden years.

The Long-Distance Lovers

When 70-year-old Evelyn's career required her to move across the country, she and her husband, Tom, faced the challenge of maintaining their relationship from a distance. Despite the physical separation, the couple made a conscious effort to remain emotionally connected through regular phone calls, video chats, and surprise visits. Their unwavering commitment to nurturing their love, even from afar, demonstrates the resilience and strength of their bond.

The Couple That Laughs Together

For 68-year-old Clara and her husband, Sam, humor has always been the cornerstone of their relationship. As they've aged together, they've continued to find joy and laughter in both the big and small moments of life. By maintaining a light-hearted perspective and not taking themselves too seriously, Clara and Sam have kept their love alive and thriving throughout the years.

In Conclusion

Nurturing and maintaining a healthy romantic relationship as you age is essential for your emotional well-being and overall happiness. By prioritizing open communication, quality time, and affection, you can keep the spark alive in your relationship, providing support and companionship for each other as you journey through your golden years together. Remember, love knows no age, and it's never too late to strengthen your bond and enjoy a fulfilling romantic relationship.

Chapter 17: The Sandwich Generation: Balancing Care for Yourself and Loved Ones

In this chapter, we'll delve into the unique challenges faced by the sandwich generation – individuals who find themselves caring for both older and younger family members simultaneously. We'll discuss strategies for balancing your own needs with those of your loved ones, as well as tips for managing the emotional, financial, and logistical aspects of caregiving.

The Challenges of the Sandwich Generation
Caring for both older and younger family members can be a complex and demanding task, with challenges that may include:

1. Emotional stress: Juggling the needs of multiple family members can lead to feelings of guilt, anxiety, and overwhelm.

2. Financial strain: Providing care for multiple generations can put a significant financial burden on the caregiver.

3. Time management: Balancing caregiving responsibilities with personal and professional obligations can be a logistical challenge.

4. Physical exhaustion: Caregiving can be physically demanding, particularly when caring for older family members with health issues or disabilities.

Strategies for Balancing Care

To navigate the challenges of the sandwich generation, consider these strategies for balancing care for yourself and your loved ones:

1. Set boundaries: Establish clear boundaries for your caregiving responsibilities and communicate these to your family members to ensure a sustainable balance.

2. Prioritize self-care: Take care of your own physical, mental, and emotional well-being to ensure you have the energy and resilience to care for others.

3. Delegate tasks: Enlist the help of other family members or hire professional caregivers to share the caregiving burden and lighten your load.

4. Create a support network: Connect with friends, support groups, or online communities to share your experiences and gain advice from others facing similar challenges.

5. Seek financial assistance: Investigate financial assistance programs and resources for caregivers to help offset the costs of caregiving.

6. Utilize respite care: Arrange for temporary respite care, either in-home or at a facility, to give yourself a much-needed break.

7. Be proactive: Anticipate the needs of your family members and plan ahead to avoid last-minute crises and stress.

Managing the Emotional Aspects of Caregiving

Caring for multiple generations can be emotionally taxing. Consider these tips for managing the emotional aspects of caregiving:

1. Practice empathy: Recognize and validate the emotions of your family members, fostering a supportive and understanding environment.

2. Develop coping strategies: Cultivate healthy coping mechanisms, such as mindfulness, exercise, or journaling, to help manage stress and emotions.

3. Communicate openly: Encourage open and honest communication within your family to address any concerns or feelings related to caregiving.

4. Seek professional help: Consider speaking with a therapist or counsellor to help you navigate the emotional challenges of caregiving.

In Conclusion

Balancing care for yourself and your loved ones can be challenging, but with the right strategies and support, you can successfully navigate the unique demands of the sandwich generation. Prioritizing self-care, setting boundaries, and creating a support network will help you maintain a sustainable balance and ensure the well-being of both you and your family members. Remember, you don't have to do it all alone – reach out for help when needed and take time to care for yourself along the way.

Chapter 18: Embracing Technology: Staying Connected in the Digital Age

In this chapter, we'll explore the importance of mastering new technologies to enhance communication and daily life in your golden years. We'll discuss the benefits of embracing technology, provide tips for overcoming the digital learning curve, and share resources to help you stay connected in the digital age.

The Benefits of Embracing Technology

Technology offers numerous benefits for older adults, including:

1. Enhanced communication: Stay connected with family and friends through video calls, social media, and messaging apps.

2. Improved access to information: Access a wealth of information on topics such as health, finance, and current events through the internet.

3. Entertainment and leisure: Enjoy movies, music, games, and other forms of digital entertainment at your fingertips.

4. Simplified daily tasks: Use technology to manage daily tasks, such as online shopping, banking, and appointment scheduling.

5. Health monitoring: Utilize digital health tools and wearables to monitor your health and maintain wellness.

Tips for Overcoming the Digital Learning Curve

If you're new to technology or feel overwhelmed by the digital world, consider these tips for overcoming the learning curve:

1. Start with the basics: Begin by mastering essential technologies, such as smartphones, tablets, or computers, and gradually build your skills from there.

2. Be patient with yourself: Recognize that learning new technology takes time and practice, so be patient and give yourself credit for your progress.

3. Seek help from others: Ask family members, friends, or community resources for assistance in learning and troubleshooting new technologies.

4. Take advantage of tutorials: Utilize online tutorials, manuals, and other resources to learn new skills and applications.

5. Join a tech class or group: Enrol in technology classes specifically designed for older adults or join a group where you can learn and practice together.

Resources for Staying Connected in the Digital Age

Here are some resources to help you stay connected and master new technologies:

1. SeniorNet: A non-profit organization offering computer and technology education to older adults, both online and through local learning canters.

2. AARP TEK (Technology Education and Knowledge): A program by AARP that provides technology education, workshops, and online resources for older adults.

3. Local libraries and community canters: Many libraries and community canters offer technology classes and workshops for older adults.

4. YouTube tutorials: Search for video tutorials on specific devices or applications to learn at your own pace.

5. Tech-savvy family and friends: Enlist the help of tech-savvy loved ones to teach you new skills or troubleshoot issues.

In Conclusion

Embracing technology is essential for staying connected and enhancing your daily life in the digital age. By overcoming the learning curve and utilizing resources designed for older adults, you can master new technologies and enjoy the many benefits they offer. Remember, it's never too late to learn and adapt to the ever-changing digital world, so be patient with yourself and celebrate your progress along the way.

Chapter 19: Mindfulness and Meditation: Cultivating Inner Peace and Resilience

In this chapter, we'll explore the benefits of practicing mindfulness and meditation in your golden years. We'll discuss how these techniques can help you cope with stress and maintain emotional well-being, and provide guidance on incorporating mindfulness practices into your daily life.

The Benefits of Mindfulness and Meditation

Mindfulness and meditation offer numerous benefits for older adults, including:

1. Stress reduction: Regular mindfulness practice can help lower stress levels by promoting relaxation and

encouraging a non-judgmental awareness of the present moment.

2. Improved emotional well-being: Mindfulness and meditation can help increase self-awareness, promote positive emotions, and enhance overall mental health.

3. Better sleep: Practicing relaxation techniques before bedtime can help improve sleep quality and combat insomnia.

4. Enhanced cognitive function: Mindfulness has been shown to improve focus, attention, and memory, which can be particularly beneficial as we age.

5. Pain management: Mindfulness techniques can help manage chronic pain by promoting relaxation and increasing awareness of bodily sensations.

Incorporating Mindfulness Practices into Your Daily Life

To cultivate inner peace and resilience, consider incorporating these mindfulness practices into your daily life:

1. Formal meditation: Set aside time each day to practice meditation, focusing on your breath, body sensations, or a specific mantra. Start with just a few minutes per day and gradually increase the duration as you become more comfortable.

2. Mindful breathing: Throughout the day, pause to take a few deep, slow breaths, focusing on the sensation of your breath as it moves in and out of your body.

3. Body scan: Perform a mental scan of your body, noting any areas of tension or discomfort, and then consciously relax those areas.

4. Mindful eating: Practice being fully present and aware during meals, savouring the taste, texture, and aroma of each bite.

5. Walking meditation: Take a slow, mindful walk, focusing on the sensation of your feet hitting the ground and the rhythm of your breath.

6. Loving-kindness meditation: Cultivate compassion and loving-kindness towards yourself and others by silently repeating phrases such as, "May I be happy, may I be healthy, may I be safe, may I be at ease."

7. Gratitude practice: Reflect on the things you are grateful for each day, either through journaling or quiet contemplation.

Getting Started with Mindfulness and Meditation

If you're new to mindfulness and meditation, consider these resources and tips to help you get started:

1. Guided meditation apps: Download a meditation app, such as Headspace, Calm, or Insight Timer, which offer guided meditations and mindfulness exercises specifically designed for beginners.

2. Local meditation groups or classes: Join a local meditation group or enroll in a class to learn from experienced instructors and practice with others.

3. Books and online resources: Explore books and online resources on mindfulness and meditation, such as "The Miracle of Mindfulness" by Thich Nhat Hanh or "Full Catastrophe Living" by Jon Kabat-Zinn.

4. Be patient and consistent: Remember that mindfulness is a skill that takes time and practice to develop. Be patient with yourself and commit to practicing consistently for the best results.

In Conclusion

Practicing mindfulness and meditation can help you cope with stress, maintain emotional well-being, and cultivate inner peace and resilience in your golden years. By incorporating mindfulness techniques into your daily life, you can foster a greater sense of self-awareness, relaxation, and overall mental health. Remember, it's never too late to start exploring mindfulness practices, and the benefits will continue to unfold as you deepen your practice over time.

Chapter 20: Conclusion: The Golden Ticket to a Fulfilling Life

As we conclude our exploration of aging gracefully, let us reflect on the journey we've taken together and the opportunities that lie ahead. Throughout this guide, we've discussed a wide range of topics and strategies designed to help you thrive in your golden years – from debunking myths about aging and embracing a healthy lifestyle, to nurturing relationships and exploring new passions.

Embracing the Golden Years

The golden years can be a time of incredible growth, adventure, and fulfilment. By embracing the wisdom, experience, and beauty that come with age, you can create a life that is rich in meaning and purpose. Remember, it's never too late to make changes, learn new skills, or pursue new interests. As you embark on this new phase of life, allow yourself to be open to new experiences and opportunities.

A Lifetime of Learning

Life is a continuous journey of learning and self-discovery, and your golden years are no exception. As you navigate this stage of life, stay curious and committed to personal growth. Seek out new knowledge, embrace change, and challenge yourself to explore new avenues of self-expression and connection. The more you learn and grow, the more vibrant and fulfilling your life will become.

The Power of Community

One of the most powerful aspects of aging gracefully is the power of community. As you continue to nurture relationships with family, friends, and community members, you'll find strength and support in the bonds you've built. Engage in intergenerational relationships, volunteer your time and talents, and seek out new friendships. By staying connected and involved, you'll not only enrich your own life but also the lives of those around you.

The Art of Balance

Lastly, remember that balance is key to a fulfilling life. By maintaining a balance between your physical, mental, emotional, and spiritual well-being, you can create a life that is both vibrant and harmonious. Listen to your body, practice self-care, and prioritize the activities and relationships that bring you joy and meaning.

Looking Ahead

As you move forward, embrace the opportunities that lie ahead with an open heart and mind. Remember that you have the power to shape your golden years into a time of growth, exploration, and joy. Continue to invest in your well-being, nurture your relationships, and pursue your passions. By doing so, you'll create a life that is not only fulfilling but also a true testament to the beauty and wisdom of aging gracefully.

In closing, we hope that this guide has inspired and empowered you to thrive in your golden years. May the journey ahead be filled with laughter, love, and countless golden moments.

About the Author

Sam Clarke is a retired entrepreneur and founder of an Ecommerce company.

With a career spanning several decades and multiple senior positions in major companies, Sam brings a wealth of experience and expertise to his writing.

His latest book, 'Aging Gracefully: A Guide to Thriving in Your Golden Years', is a product of his passion for helping others enjoy their retirement.

Inspired by his friend, bestselling author Sally Mooney, Sam has written this guide to share his knowledge and insights with those who are thinking about retiring or have already retired

Hope you enjoy!

Check out Sally's books on Amazon:

The Illustrated Book of Funny Old Sayings

The Illustrated Book of Odd Little Sayings

The Egg Cookbook for Kids: Easy and fun recipes for kids to make

Chicken Chook: A Greedy bird that likes to cook

Chicken Chook: So many eggs

© 2023 by Sam Clarke

ISBN: 9798391955085

All Rights Reserved.   No part of this publication may be reproduced in any form or by any means, including scanning, photocopying, or otherwise without prior written permission of the copyright holder.

First Printing, 2023

Printed in the United States of America

Printed in Great Britain
by Amazon